Introducing Marvello the Great

Amazing Magical

JELL-O Desserts

BRAND

Contents

Holiday
Desserts
page 76

Party
Desserts
page 89

Making Magic with Jell-O® Brand Desserts.

This is a book about magic and making magic — the magic of your family having fun together, building memories and traditions. And, we know you'll agree that it's fun to make magic both for and with your children with the exciting Jell-O brand dessert recipes in this book.

Do you remember the first thing that you cooked and what fun it was? Maybe it was cookies or popcorn. Probably it was Jell-O brand gelatin. Remember stirring the red powder very carefully with your wooden spoon until it was all dissolved? What magic! Millions of children first cooked by helping their mothers make Jell-O brand gelatin and pudding.

Now, you find yourself teaching many of the same things to your children. This book was written to help you carry on that tradition.

HOW TO USE THIS BOOK.

The recipes are presented in a new, clear style. First, we tell you that *These Go In*, and we list all the foods you need in preparing the recipe. Next, we tell you to *Get These Ready*, and we put down every pot or spoon or mold you need; and there are drawings of the utensils so that even your youngest child who can't read can help you cook.

Some of the Jell-O brand gelatin and pudding recipes are very easy to make and preschoolers can do them under your supervision. These are marked with a ♥ so that you will be able to spot them right away. Other recipes are a little more challenging and will appeal to the interests of older children. These are marked with a ◆ And when you see a ★, you'll know that these recipes are for children with more cooking skills. But none of the recipes is hard; none makes use of any bowl or mold or cutter that you don't have right now in your kitchen. And, best of all, each recipe is fun and delicious.

And there's another kind of magic in these pages, too. A funny fellow named Marvello tells us about magic tricks that the kids can perform. Get ready for a show! And on the bottom corners of each page, there are pictures that move when you flip the pages with your thumb. Flip the pages forward, and you'll see a Jell-O brand gelatin dessert disappear. Flip the pages backwards, and you'll see a rabbit coming out of the hat!

How to Make Jell-O Brand Gelatin.

1. Add 1 cup boiling water to gelatin in a bowl.
2. Stir until completely dissolved.
3. Stir in 1 cup cold water.
4. Chill until set.
   Makes 2 cups or 4 servings.

To add other ingredients:
Fold ¾ to 1½ cups fruits or vegetables into slightly thickened gelatin, chill until set.
(Do *not* add fresh or frozen pineapple.)

To mold gelatin:
Decrease cold water to ¾ cup.
Pour into mold and chill until firm.
To unmold, see helpful hints below.

HELPFUL HINTS FOR MAKING JELL-O BRAND GELATIN.
For speed setting:
Use a metal mold or bowl rather than one made of glass.
Substitute 2 cups of ice cubes for the cup of cold water.
Stir until the gelatin starts to thicken; then remove any unmelted ice.
Or, substitute 1 cup crushed ice or ice cubes and water; then stir until ice is completely melted.

Layering:
Each layer must be set, but not firm, before you add the next layer. If it is too firm, the top layer will slip off when it is unmolded. Let the gelatin chill to the point where it will stick to your finger when you touch it and moves gently from side to side when the bowl is tilted. When this happens, you can add the next layer.

Unmolding:
No need to be nervous when you unmold a gelatin dessert. Just follow these directions:

The gelatin must be firm. It should not move when you tilt the bowl from side to side.

Run a spatula, knife or moistened finger around the top edge, between the gelatin and mold.

Dip the mold in warm water for 10 seconds...all the way up to the rim.

Remove mold from the water and shake gently to loosen the gelatin.

Place a moistened plate on top of the mold.

Turn the plate and mold upside down together, shake the mold onto the plate and lift the mold right off.

If it doesn't work the first time, DON'T WORRY; just dip the mold in water and shake it again.

How to Make Jell-O Brand Pudding.

1. Mix pudding with 2 cups milk in a saucepan.
2. Cook and stir over medium heat until mixture comes to a boil. Pudding will thicken as it cools. Serve warm or cold. Makes 2 cups or 4 servings.
   For pie:
   Cook and stir to a *full bubbling* boil. Let stand 5 minutes, stirring twice. Pour into a baked, cooled 8-inch pie shell. Chill 3 hours.

HELPFUL HINTS FOR MAKING JELL-O BRAND PUDDING.

Pudding must be stirred *constantly* as it cooks and must come to a *boil*. It will be thin, but remember pudding thickens as it cools.

If cooking is interrupted, remove from heat for as long as 15 minutes, then return to heat and bring to a boil as directed.

For creamier pudding:
Cover bowl with plastic wrap while pudding cools; stir before serving.

Instead of whole milk you can use:
Skim milk;
Reconstituted evaporated milk;
Reconstituted nonfat dry milk.

How to Make Jell-O Brand Instant Pudding

For pudding recipes:
1. Pour 2 cups *cold* milk into bowl. Add pudding mix.
2. Beat slowly with hand beater or use electric mixer at lowest speed until mixture is well blended, about 2 minutes.
3. Pour into dessert dishes right away. Pudding will be soft set and ready to eat in 5 minutes. Makes 2 cups or 4 servings.

For pie recipes:
Follow directions for pudding but:

1. Decrease amount of cold milk to 1¾ cups.
2. Beat mixture only 1 minute to blend. (Mixture will be thin.)
3. Pour into baked, cooled 8-inch pie shell right away. Chill at least 1 hour.

HELPFUL HINTS FOR MAKING JELL-O BRAND INSTANT PUDDING.
Using a shaker:
Pour milk into 1-quart leakproof container, such as a glass quart jar or plastic freezer container.
Add pudding mix and cover tightly.
Shake *vigorously* for at least 30 seconds.

Using a fork:
Pour milk into 1½-quart bowl.
Add pudding mix.
Stir with a fork for 3 minutes.

Family Desserts.

The evening meal can be a fun time for the family. Add your own special magic with desserts made with Jell-O brand gelatin and pudding.

◆Peach Slope

THESE GO IN:
1 package (3 oz.) Jell-O brand
  peach flavor gelatin
1 cup boiling water
1 can (8¾ oz.) sliced peaches
1 cup Birds Eye Cool Whip
  non-dairy whipped topping

GET THESE READY:
2 mixing bowls
  1-cup liquid measure
  strainer
  mixing spoon
  wire whip (optional)
5 parfait glasses

HOW TO MAKE IT:
1. Dissolve gelatin in boiling water.
2. Drain peaches, reserving syrup.
   Add water to syrup to make 1 cup.
3. Add measured liquid to gelatin,
   measure 1 cup and set aside.
4. Pour remaining gelatin into 5
   parfait glasses; place 2 or 3
   peach slices in each glass.
5. Tilt glasses in refrigerator.
   (Place the bases between two
   bars of shelf and carefully lean
   sides against the wall.) Chill
   until set.
6. Meanwhile, chill measured
   gelatin until slightly thickened;
   then fold in whipped topping.
   Spoon over set gelatin in
   glasses and chill upright until
   set, about 1 hour.
7. Garnish with additional
   whipped topping and peach
   slices, if desired. Makes about
   3 cups or 5 servings.

♥ Sink or Swim

THESE GO IN:
1 package (3 oz.) Jell-O brand strawberry flavor gelatin
1 cup boiling water
1 cup cold water or ginger ale
1 cup (about) fruit combination*

Fruits that sink: Mandarin oranges; seedless grapes; drained canned fruits (packed in heavy syrup) such as: peach slices, sliced pear halves, crushed pineapple or pineapple chunks, cherries or apricots.

Fruits that float: Banana slices; apple wedges or diced apple; strawberry halves; fresh orange sections; fresh sliced peaches or pears; marshmallows or coarsely chopped nuts.

GET THESE READY:
mixing bowl
1-cup liquid measure
mixing spoon
1-cup dry measure

HOW TO MAKE IT:
1. Dissolve gelatin in boiling water in heatproof glass bowl. Add cold water.
2. Add fruits that will sink; then add fruits that float.
3. Chill until firm, at least 3 hours. Garnish with thawed Birds Eye Cool Whip non-dairy whipped topping, if desired. Makes 5 servings.

♥ Magic Chocolate Peak

THESE GO IN:
1 package (4-serving size) Jell-O brand chocolate flavor pudding and pie filling
2 cups milk
1 pint vanilla ice cream

GET THESE READY:
saucepan
rubber scraper
1-cup liquid measure
ice cream scoop
6 to 8 dessert dishes

HOW TO MAKE IT:
1. Prepare pudding mix with milk as directed, on package .
2. Immediately pour hot pudding into dishes and top with scoops of ice cream. (Or, pour hot pudding over scoops of ice cream.) Serve at once. Makes 6 to 8 servings.

♥Ship Ahoy

THESE GO IN:
1 package (3 oz.) Jell-O brand
  gelatin, any flavor
1 cup boiling water
1 cup cold water
4 wedge-shaped pieces of fruit
  (drained pear halves, peach
  slices, grapefruit or orange
  sections, or quartered banana)

GET THESE READY:
1 mixing bowl
  1-cup liquid measure
  mixing spoon
4 dessert dishes
  white paper
  wooden picks

HOW TO MAKE IT:
1. Dissolve gelatin in boiling water.
   Add cold water and pour into 4
   individual dessert dishes. Chill
   until set but not firm, about
   1½ hours.
2. Cut 4 small triangles from white
   paper to make sails. Insert
   wooden picks through "sails"
   and secure to fruit pieces.
3. Place on set gelatin; chill until
   firm. Makes 2 cups or 4
   servings.
   Note: Dip banana in lemon
   juice to prevent darkening.

◆Peanut Butter Fluff

THESE GO IN:
2 cups cold milk
½ cup chunky peanut butter
1 package (4-serving size)
  Jell-O brand chocolate fudge
  flavor instant pudding
  and pie filling
1 cup thawed Birds Eye Cool
  Whip non-dairy whipped
  topping

GET THESE READY:
small mixing bowl
electric mixer or
  hand beater
1-cup liquid measure
rubber scraper
1-cup and ½-cup
  dry measures
tablespoon
6 dessert dishes

HOW TO MAKE IT:
1. Gradually blend milk into peanut butter in a bowl.
2. Add pudding mix, beat slowly with hand beater or at lowest speed of electric mixer until well blended, about 2 minutes.
3. Fold in whipped topping and spoon into individual dessert dishes.
4. Arrange halved peanuts on pudding to make a face, if desired. Makes about 3 cups or 6 servings.

♦Apricot Silly Face

THESE GO IN:
1 package (3 oz.) Jell-O brand
 apricot flavor gelatin
1¼ cups boiling water
1 cup vanilla ice cream
1 jar (4¾ oz.) strained apricots
 with tapioca

GET THESE READY:
mixing bowl
1-cup liquid measure
1-cup dry measure
mixing spoon
5 dessert dishes

HOW TO MAKE IT:
1. Dissolve gelatin in boiling water.

2. Add ice cream by spoonfuls, stirring until blended and smooth.
3. Fold in apricots and pour into dessert dishes.
4. Chill until set, about 1 hour. Arrange chocolate chips to resemble faces and chocolate wafers and marshmallows for hats, if desired. Makes 2¾ cups or 5 servings.

◆Magic Stripe Parfait

THESE GO IN:
1 package (3 oz.) Jell-O brand cherry, strawberry, raspberry or lime flavor gelatin
1 cup boiling water
1 cup cold water
Light cream, half and half or milk

GET THESE READY:
1-cup liquid measure
mixing bowl
mixing spoon
4 parfait glasses
drinking straw

HOW TO MAKE IT:
1. Dissolve gelatin in boiling water; add cold water.
2. Pour into parfait glasses, filling each to about 1 inch from the top. Chill until firm.
3. Pour cream over top of set gelatin, about ½ inch deep.
4. Using a drinking straw, make deep tunnels at intervals around outside and through center of gelatin, allowing cream to settle into the tunnels. Makes about 2 cups or 4 servings.

◆Clear and Cloudy

THESE GO IN:
1 package (3 oz.) Jell-O brand strawberry or apricot flavor gelatin
1 cup boiling water
¾ cup cold water
2 tablespoons strawberry or apricot preserves
½ cup thawed Birds Eye Cool Whip non-dairy whipped topping

GET THESE READY:
2 mixing bowls
1-cup liquid measure
mixing spoon
measuring spoons
½-cup dry measure
4 parfait glasses

HOW TO MAKE IT:
1. Dissolve gelatin in boiling water. Measure ¼ cup and set aside.
2. Add cold water to remaining gelatin and chill until thickened.
3. Meanwhile, add preserves to measured gelatin. Chill until slightly thickened; then fold in whipped topping.
4. Spoon clear and creamy mixtures alternately into 4 parfait glasses.
5. Place a small paper parasol in each dessert, if desired. Makes about 2 cups or 4 servings.

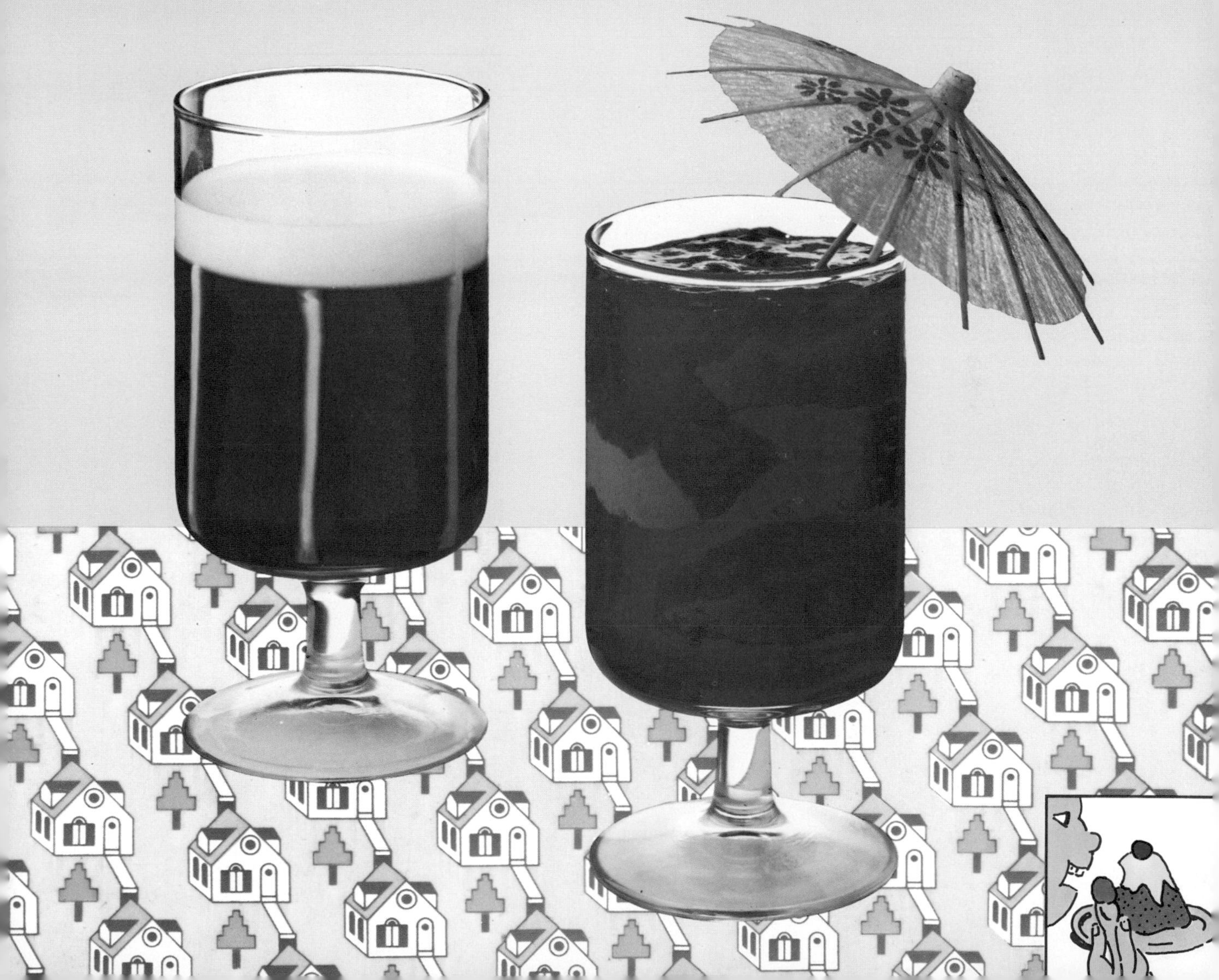

★Funny Lemon Freeze

THESE GO IN:
1 package (3 oz.) Jell-O brand lemon flavor gelatin
¼ cup sugar
1 cup boiling water
1 cup cold water
1 can (6 oz.) frozen concentrate for lemonade
2 teaspoons grated lemon rind
1 envelope Dream Whip whipped topping mix
2 egg whites
¼ cup sugar

GET THESE READY:
large mixing bowl
2 small mixing bowls
rubber scraper
¼-cup dry measure
1-cup liquid measure
measuring spoons
hand beater or electric mixer
9-inch square pan
dessert dishes

HOW TO MAKE IT:
1. Dissolve gelatin and ¼ cup sugar in boiling water.
2. Add cold water, frozen concentrate and lemon rind. Chill until slightly thickened.
3. Prepare whipped topping mix as directed on package.
4. Beat egg whites until foamy. Gradually beat in ¼ cup sugar and continue beating until mixture will form stiff, shiny peaks.
5. Fold in gelatin; then fold in whipped topping, blending well.
6. Pour into a 9-inch square pan. Freeze until firm, about 4 hours or overnight.
7. Scoop onto flattened paper baking cups, top with ice-cream cones and decorate with gumdrops, if desired. Makes about 6 cups or 10 to 12 servings.

Marvello's Ball Game

YOU'LL NEED:

1 small rubber ball (a jacks ball would be good)
1 large white man's handkerchief
  or
1 square silky scarf
needle
thread

Here's a funny way to begin your magic show. Take a big white handkerchief or a silky scarf and sew the rubber ball (remember it has to be a small one) in the center. Tuck the handkerchief into your pocket, but be sure to leave the ends fluttering out. As soon as you have stepped in front of your audience and bowed, pull the handkerchief out of your pocket and wipe your forehead with it; then drop it casually to the floor in front of you. With a little practice, you'll be able to drop the ball just hard enough so that it will bounce right back into your hand, and you can return it calmly to your pocket.

◆Banana Wobbler

THESE GO IN:
1 package (3 oz.) Jell-O brand
    gelatin, any flavor
1 cup boiling water
½ cup cold water
2 medium bananas,
    cut in half
  Lemon juice
  Shoestring licorice

GET THESE READY:
3 empty 6-ounce juice cans
  mixing bowl
1-cup liquid measure
  mixing spoon
  paring knife

HOW TO MAKE IT:
1. Dissolve gelatin in boiling water. Add cold water and chill until thickened.
2. Place a spoonful of gelatin in each of 3 empty 6-ounce cans.
3. Center the banana halves and spoon remaining gelatin around bananas.
4. Chill until firm, about 2 hours. (Dip remaining banana half in lemon juice; set aside for another dessert.)
5. Dip each can to the rim in warm water, invert onto plate, puncture bottom and lift off can.
6. Insert piece of licorice in one end of each mold to resemble firecracker. Makes 3 servings.

★Crisscross Banana Cream Pie

THESE GO IN:
1 large banana, sliced
1 baked 9-inch pie shell, cooled
1 package (6-serving size) Jell-O brand banana cream or vanilla flavor instant pudding and pie filling
2½ cups cold milk
1 cup thawed Birds Eye Cool Whip non-dairy whipped topping

GET THESE READY:
paring knife
9-inch pie plate
electric mixer or hand beater
small mixing bowl
2-cup liquid measure
1-cup dry measure
rubber scraper
pastry bag with lettering tube

HOW TO MAKE IT:
1. Arrange banana slices in bottom of pie shell.
2. Prepare pie filling mix with milk as directed on package for pie.
3. Pour at once into pie shell. Chill 3 hours.
4. Using pastry bag with lettering tube, garnish with whipped topping, additional banana slices and gumdrops to resemble a game of tic-tac-toe, if desired.

♥Ambrosia Pudding

THESE GO IN:
1 package (4-serving size) Jell-O brand coconut cream flavor instant pudding and pie filling
2 cups cold milk
1 can (11 oz.) mandarin orange sections, drained
½ teaspoon grated orange rind (optional)

GET THESE READY:
hand beater or electric mixer

small mixing bowl
strainer
mixing spoon
1-cup liquid measure
grater
measuring spoons
dessert glasses or bowl

HOW TO MAKE IT:
1. Prepare pudding mix with milk as directed on package for pudding.
2. Fold in orange sections and orange rind, reserving a few sections for garnish, if desired
3. Pour into individual dessert glasses or a serving bowl and chill. Garnish with reserved sections and mint sprigs, if desired. Makes about 2½ cups or 5 servings.

Ambrosia Pudding Mousse:
Prepare Ambrosia Pudding as directed, decreasing milk to 1½ cups and folding in 1 cup thawed Birds Eye Cool Whip non-dairy whipped topping. Makes about 2⅔ cups or 5 servings.

♥Sunny Whip

THESE GO IN:
1 package (3 oz.) Jell-O brand
  orange flavor gelatin
1 cup boiling water
¾ cup cold orange juice

GET THESE READY:
mixing bowl
1-cup liquid measure
mixing spoon
hand beater or
  electric mixer
rubber scraper
6 dessert glasses

HOW TO MAKE IT:
1. Dissolve gelatin in boiling water.
   Add orange juice.
2. Chill until slightly thickened;
   then whip with hand beater or
   electric mixer until fluffy and
   thick, about double in
   volume.
3. Spoon into dessert glasses;
   chill.
4. Garnish with halved orange
   slices, decorated with cloves
   and maraschino cherries, if
   desired. Makes 4 cups or 6
   servings.

◆ Icy Chocolate Apricot Dessert

THESE GO IN:

1 package (3 oz.) Jell-O brand apricot flavor gelatin
1 cup boiling water
2 cups ice cubes
1 cup thawed Birds Eye Cool Whip non-dairy whipped topping
½ cup chocolate cookie crumbs

GET THESE READY:
mixing bowl
1-cup liquid measure
mixing spoon
1-cup dry measure
½-cup dry measure
wire whip

4 dessert glasses

HOW TO MAKE IT:

1. Dissolve gelatin in boiling water.
2. Add ice cubes and stir until gelatin begins to thicken, 3 to 5 minutes.
3. Remove any unmelted ice. Measure 1 cup gelatin; set aside.
4. Blend whipped topping into remaining gelatin.
5. Spoon half the creamy gelatin mixture into glasses. Top with the cookie crumbs.
6. Spoon in remaining creamy mixture; chill until set, about 30 minutes. Top with reserved clear gelatin. Chill. Add a paper sign, if desired. Makes 3¼ cups or 4 or 5 servings.

DANGER THIN ICE

♥Jiffy Sauce

THESE GO IN:
¾ cup corn syrup
1 package (4-serving size)
  Jell-O brand butterscotch,
  chocolate, or chocolate fudge
  flavor instant pudding and pie
  filling
¾ cup evaporated milk or light
  cream

GET THESE READY:
1-cup liquid measure
mixing bowl
mixing spoon

HOW TO MAKE IT:
1. Pour corn syrup into bowl.
   Blend in pudding mix.
2. Gradually add evaporated milk,
   stirring constantly. Let stand
   10 minutes.
3. Serve over ice cream or cake.
   Makes about 2 cups.
   Note: Sauce may be stored in
   covered container in refrigerator
   for a week.

◆Great Pecan Pie

THESE GO IN:

1 package (4-serving size) Jell-O brand butter pecan flavor instant pudding and pie filling
1 cup light or dark corn syrup
¾ cup evaporated milk
1 egg, slightly beaten
½ cup chopped pecans
1 unbaked 8-inch pie shell

GET THESE READY:

8-inch pie plate
mixing bowl
1-cup liquid measure
fork or wire whip
mixing spoon
½-cup dry measure
rubber scraper
cake rack
pot holders
knife

HOW TO MAKE IT:

1. Combine pie filling mix and corn syrup in bowl.
2. Gradually add evaporated milk and egg, blending well.
3. Add pecans and pour into pie shell.
4. Bake at 375° until top is firm and just begins to crack, about 45 to 50 minutes.
5. Cool at least 3 hours before cutting.
6. Garnish with thawed Birds Eye Cool Whip non-dairy whipped topping and pecan halves, if desired.

◆ Surprise Bottom Pie

THESE GO IN:
1 unbaked 8-inch pie shell
⅓ cup Baker's chocolate flavor baking chips
1 package (4-serving size) Jell-O brand vanilla or butter pecan flavor instant pudding and pie filling

GET THESE READY:
8-inch pie plate 🍽

⅓-cup dry measure
metal spatula
hand beater or electric mixer
small mixing bowl
1-cup liquid measure
rubber scraper
teaspoon

HOW TO MAKE IT:
1. Bake pie shell at 425° for 12 to 15 minutes, or until lightly browned. Remove from oven.
2. *Immediately* sprinkle chips in single layer on bottom of pie shell.
3. Let stand 3 to 5 minutes to melt chips; then spread evenly over bottom and sides of crust. Cool thoroughly.
4. Meanwhile, prepare pie filling mix as directed on package for pie.
5. Pour at once into chocolate-coated crust. Chill 1 hour. Garnish with thawed Birds Eye Cool Whip non-dairy whipped topping and additional chocolate chips, if desired.

Marvello's
Pick and Choose Trick

YOU'LL NEED:

1 person to assist you

In this trick you're going to show that you're a mind reader!
You and your partner will decide, in advance, how the trick will
be done. First, your partner is sent out of the room while the
audience picks out an object (or objects) for him to guess. The
object can be anything in the room.

When the partner is called back, he is supposed to guess the
object(s) that was chosen. You begin by pointing to different
things in the room asking "Is it this?" If you point to the wrong
thing, your partner says "No"; and when you point to the correct
thing, he answers "Yes."

Here's how to do the trick. There are two ways, and to make the
audience most confused and to make yourself look really good,
you should use both of these methods. First, you can decide
with your partner ahead of time that the chosen object will be
the third or fourth thing that you will point to. Or (and this is a
little trickier), you can decide that the chosen object will be the
first thing you point to *after* you point to something red. Just be
sure that you have something red in the room and point to it
just before you point to the chosen object.

♥Cherry Cola Cooler

THESE GO IN:
1 package (3 oz.) Jell-O brand cherry flavor gelatin
1 cup boiling water
1 cup cola beverage

GET THESE READY:
mixing bowl
1-cup liquid measure
mixing spoon
4 small glasses

HOW TO MAKE IT:
1. Dissolve gelatin in boiling water. Add cola beverage.
2. Pour into small soda glasses or individual dessert dishes.
3. Chill until set, about 1 hour. Garnish with thawed Birds Eye Cool Whip non-dairy whipped topping and maraschino cherries, if desired. Makes about 2 cups or 4 servings.

◆Strawberry Yogurt Poof

THESE GO IN:
1 package (3 oz.) Jell-O brand
  strawberry flavor gelatin
1 cup boiling water
¾ cup cold water
1 container (8 oz.) strawberry
  yogurt

GET THESE READY:
mixing bowl
1-cup liquid measure
rubber scraper
hand beater
large spoon
8 dessert dishes

HOW TO MAKE IT:
1. Dissolve gelatin in boiling water;
   add cold water and chill until
   slightly thickened.
2. Add yogurt and beat with hand
   beater until mixture is light and
   fluffy.
3. Pour into individual dishes.
   Chill until firm, about 2 hours.
   Garnish with names, using
   Post Alpha-Bits cereal, if
   desired. Makes 4 cups or 8
   servings.

♥Peach Float

THESE GO IN:
1 package (3 oz.) Jell-O brand
  peach or orange flavor gelatin
1 cup boiling water
1 can (16 oz.) peach halves
5 or 6 maraschino cherries, drained

GET THESE READY:
2 mixing bowls
  strainer
  1-cup liquid measure
  mixing spoon
5 or 6 dessert dishes

HOW TO MAKE IT:
1. Dissolve gelatin in boiling water.
2. Drain peaches, reserving syrup. Add water to syrup, if necessary, to make 1 cup.
3. Add measured liquid to gelatin and chill until slightly thickened.
4. Pour into dessert dishes. Place one peach half, cut side up, in each dish; place one cherry in each peach cavity.
5. Chill until firm, about 3 hours. Makes 5 or 6 servings.

♥Pudding Swirl

THESE GO IN:
1 package (4-serving size)
  Jell-O brand chocolate or
  chocolate fudge flavor instant
  pudding and pie filling
2 cups cold milk
1 cup thawed Birds Eye Cool
  Whip non-dairy whipped
  topping

GET THESE READY:
small mixing bowl
electric mixer or
    hand beater
2-cup liquid measure
1-cup dry measure
rubber scraper
spoon
6 dessert glasses

HOW TO MAKE IT:
1. Prepare pudding mix with milk
   as directed on package. Let
   stand for 5 minutes.
2. Fold whipped topping into
   pudding for a marbled effect.
   Spoon into dessert glasses.
   Chill. Makes about 3 cups or
   6 servings.

♥Sundae Supreme

bowl
spoon
4 sundae glasses

THESE GO IN:
1 package (4-serving size) Jell-O brand vanilla or butter pecan flavor pudding and pie filling
2 cups cold milk
   Chocolate or butterscotch sundae sauce or fruit sauce

GET THESE READY:
saucepan
1-cup liquid measure

HOW TO MAKE IT:
1. Prepare pudding mix with milk as directed on package for pudding; chill.
2. Spoon into individual dessert or sundae glasses.
3. Top with sauce. Garnish with thawed Birds Eye Cool Whip non-dairy whipped topping, chopped nuts and maraschino cherries, if desired. Makes 2 cups or 4 servings.

◆Sunken Treasure

THESE GO IN:
1 package (3 oz.) Jell-O brand
orange flavor gelatin
1 cup boiling water
¾ cup cold water
1 can (8¾ oz.) fruit cocktail,
drained
¼ cup prepared Dream Whip
whipped topping*
 *Or use thawed Birds Eye Cool
Whip non-dairy whipped
topping.

GET THESE READY:
mixing bowl
1-cup liquid measure
mixing spoon
8- or 9-inch square pan
table fork
4 or 5 dessert glasses
teaspoon

HOW TO MAKE IT:
1. Dissolve gelatin in boiling water.
   Add cold water.
2. Pour into an 8- or 9-inch square
   pan. Chill until firm, about 3
   hours.
3. Break into small flakes with a
   fork.
4. Spoon one third of the flaked
   gelatin into 4 or 5 individual
   dessert glasses.
5. Add a layer of fruit to each glass.
6. Blend whipped topping into
   another third of the flaked
   gelatin and spoon into glasses.
   Garnish with remaining flaked
   gelatin. Makes 2½ cups or 4
   or 5 servings.

♥Sunnyside Fluff

THESE GO IN:
1 can (8 oz.) sliced pineapple in juice
1 package (4-serving size) Jell-O brand lemon flavor instant pudding and pie filling
1 cup cold milk
1 cup thawed Birds Eye Cool Whip non-dairy whipped topping
8 to 10 cloves
1 or 2 maraschino cherries, sliced

GET THESE READY:
hand beater or electric mixer
small mixing bowl
rubber scraper
1-cup liquid measure
strainer
1-cup dry measure
mixing spoon
paring knife
4 dessert glasses

HOW TO MAKE IT:
1. Drain pineapple; cut 2 slices in half and cut remaining slices in small pieces.
2. Prepare pudding mix with 1 cup milk as directed on package.
3. Fold pineapple pieces and juice into pudding; then fold in whipped topping. Spoon into dessert glasses; chill.
4. Garnish with half slices of pineapple; add cloves and cherry slices to resemble eyes and mouths. Makes 2½ cups or 4 servings.

◆ Quickie Chocolate Cake

THESE GO IN:
1 package (2-layer size) chocolate cake mix
1 package (4-serving size) Jell-O brand chocolate flavor instant pudding and pie filling
4 eggs
1¼ cups water
1 cup Baker's chocolate flavor baking chips*
¼ cup oil
 *Or use 6 squares Baker's semi-sweet chocolate, coarsely chopped.

GET THESE READY:
13x9-inch pan
1-cup liquid measure
1-cup dry measure
fork
cake rack
pot holders
knife

HOW TO MAKE IT:
1. Combine all ingredients in a 13x9-inch pan and stir with a fork until blended, about 2 minutes.
2. Bake at 350° for 40 to 45 minutes, or until cake springs back when lightly pressed.
3. Cool in pan on cake rack. Sprinkle with confectioners sugar, if desired, and cut into squares. Makes 12 to 15 servings.

◆Apricot Angel

THESE GO IN:
1 package (3 oz.) Jell-O brand orange or apricot flavor gelatin
¼ teaspoon salt
1 cup boiling water
1 can (17 oz.) apricot halves
½ teaspoon grated orange rind
1 cup prepared Dream Whip whipped topping

GET THESE READY:
small bowl
strainer
1-cup liquid measure
knife
large bowl
measuring spoons
1-cup dry measure
hand beater or electric mixer
rubber scraper
tablespoon
6 or 7 dessert glasses

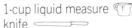

HOW TO MAKE IT:
1. Dissolve gelatin and salt in boiling water.
2. Drain apricots, reserving syrup. Add water to syrup to make ¾ cup.
3. Chop the apricots, reserving a few halves for garnish, if desired.
4. Add measured liquid and orange rind to gelatin.
5. Place bowl of gelatin in larger bowl of ice and water. Stir until slightly thickened; then whip with hand beater or electric mixer until fluffy and thick, about double in volume.
6. Fold in whipped topping; stir in chopped apricots and spoon into individual dessert glasses.
7. Chill until set, at least 1 hour. Garnish with additional whipped topping and reserved apricots. Makes about 5 cups or 6 to 7 servings.

★Terrific Trifle

THESE GO IN:

1 package (3 oz.) Jell-O brand strawberry or raspberry flavor gelatin
1 cup boiling water
1 cup cold water
1 or 2 bananas, sliced
1 sponge cake layer
¼ cup orange juice
1 package (4-serving size) Jell-O brand vanilla flavor instant pudding and pie filling
2 cups cold milk
1 cup prepared Dream Whip whipped topping or thawed Birds Eye Cool Whip non-dairy whipped topping (optional)

GET THESE READY:

mixing bowl
1-cup liquid measure
rubber scraper
paring knife
large spoon
knife
shallow serving bowl

hand beater or electric mixer
1-cup dry measure
pastry bag with tube

HOW TO MAKE IT:

1. Dissolve gelatin in boiling water. Add cold water and chill until thickened. Add bananas.
2. Split cake horizontally, making 2 layers. Place one layer in shallow serving bowl; sprinkle with half the orange juice.
3. Pour gelatin mixture over cake; top with second cake layer and sprinkle with remaining orange juice. Chill until firm, about 2 hours.
4. Prepare pudding mix with milk as directed on package for pudding.
5. Fold in whipped topping. Spoon over cake. Chill.
6. Garnish with tic-tac-toe design, using pastry bag with tube and additional prepared whipped topping and fresh fruit, if desired. Makes 8 to 10 servings.

◆Jellied Joker

THESE GO IN:
2 packages (3 oz. each) Jell-O brand peach flavor gelatin
2 cups boiling water
1 jar (17 oz.) fruits for salad

GET THESE READY:
mixing bowl
1- or 2-cup liquid measure

mixing spoon
strainer
8-inch layer pan

HOW TO MAKE IT:
1. Dissolve gelatin in boiling water.
2. Drain fruits, reserving syrup. Add water to syrup to make 1½ cups.
3. Add measured liquid to gelatin and pour 1 cup into an 8-inch layer pan. Chill until set but not firm.
4. Arrange fruits on gelatin to resemble a face. Pour about ½ cup gelatin around fruits.
5. Chill a few minutes until set and pour on remaining gelatin. Chill until firm, about 3 hours.
6. Unmold on serving plate. Cut in wedges and serve with any remaining fruits. Makes about 4½ cups or 8 servings.

◆Enchanted Chocolate-Cherry

THESE GO IN:
- 1 package (3 oz.) Jell-O brand cherry flavor gelatin
- 1 cup boiling water
- 3 tablespoons cold water
- 1½ cups chocolate ice cream
- ½ cup prepared Dream Whip whipped topping*
- ¼ cup chocolate syrup
  *Or use ½ cup thawed Birds Eye Cool Whip non-dairy whipped topping.

GET THESE READY:
mixing bowl
1-cup liquid measure
measuring spoons
rubber scraper

1-cup dry measure
½-cup dry measure
4 dessert glasses

HOW TO MAKE IT:
1. Dissolve gelatin in boiling water. Measure ¼ cup, add cold water and set aside.
2. Blend ice cream into remaining gelatin and spoon into 4 dessert glasses. Chill until set but not firm.
3. Spoon reserved gelatin over creamy gelatin in glasses. Chill until set.
4. Top each dessert with a dollop of whipped topping and drizzle with chocolate syrup. Garnish with maraschino cherries, if desired. Makes about 2½ cups or 4 or 5 servings.

◆ Lemon Honey Yummy

THESE GO IN:

1 package (3 oz.) Jell-O brand lemon flavor gelatin
1¼ cups boiling water
⅓ cup honey
3 tablespoons lemon juice
1 teaspoon grated lemon rind
1 envelope Dream Whip whipped topping mix
⅔ cup vanilla wafer crumbs

GET THESE READY:
mixing bowl
1-cup liquid measure
measuring spoons
rubber scraper
grater
electric mixer with small bowl
hand beater
8-inch square pan
8 dessert plates

HOW TO MAKE IT:

1. Dissolve gelatin in boiling water.
2. Stir in honey, lemon juice and rind; chill until slightly thickened.
3. Prepare whipped topping mix as directed on package.
4. Beat gelatin with hand beater until fluffy; then fold in whipped topping.
5. Spread half the crumbs in bottom of an 8-inch square pan.
6. Spoon in gelatin mixture and sprinkle with remaining crumbs.
7. Chill until firm, about 3 hours. Cut into squares. Garnish with twisted lemon slices, if desired. Makes about 4½ cups or 8 servings.

◆Astounding Peach Pie

THESE GO IN:
1 cup pie crust mix
1 can (16 oz.) sliced peaches*
1 package (4-serving size)
  Jell-O brand vanilla, coconut
  cream or butterscotch flavor
  pudding and pie filling
½ teaspoon ground allspice
¼ cup milk
 *Or use 1 can (17 oz.) apricot
 halves.

GET THESE READY:
8-inch pie plate

strainer
small bowl
measuring spoons
1-cup liquid measure
1-cup dry measure
paring knife
cutting board
mixing spoon
pot holders
cake rack

HOW TO MAKE IT:
1. Sprinkle ½ cup of the pie crust mix over the bottom of an 8-inch pie plate.
2. Drain peaches, reserving syrup. Set aside a few slices for garnish, if desired; dice remaining peaches.
3. Combine pudding mix, allspice, reserved syrup and the milk, blending well.
4. Stir in diced peaches and spoon half the pudding mixture over the pie crust mix.
5. Sprinkle with remaining pie crust mix and top with remaining pudding mixture.
6. Bake at 375° for 45 minutes or until set. Garnish with thawed Birds Eye Cool Whip non-dairy whipped topping and reserved peaches, if desired.
Makes 6 to 8 servings.

◆Triple Treat Parfait

THESE GO IN:
1 package (3 oz.) Jell-O brand lime flavor gelatin
1 cup boiling water
1 cup cold water
1 or 2 drops peppermint extract
1 cup thawed Birds Eye Cool Whip non-dairy whipped topping
1 package (4-serving size) Jell-O brand chocolate flavor instant pudding and pie filling
2 cups cold milk

GET THESE READY:
1 mixing bowl
1-cup liquid measure
mixing spoon
hand beater
tablespoon
8 parfait glasses

HOW TO MAKE IT:
1. Dissolve gelatin in boiling water. Add cold water and extract.
2. Pour into 8 parfait glasses, filling each about one-third full. Chill until set.
3. Spoon whipped topping into glasses, using about 2 tablespoons for each.
4. Prepare pudding mix with milk as directed on package for pudding.
5. Spoon carefully into glasses over topping. Chill at least 30 minutes.
6. Garnish with additional whipped topping and chocolate mints, if desired. Makes 4½ cups or 8 servings.

◆Poke Cake

THESE GO IN:

1 package (2-layer size) white cake mix
1 package (4-serving size) Jell-O brand vanilla flavor instant pudding and pie filling
4 eggs
1 cup water
¼ cup oil
1 package (3 oz.) Jell-O brand raspberry flavor gelatin
1 cup boiling water
1 cup cold water

GET THESE READY:

1-cup liquid measure
electric mixer
large mixer bowl
rubber scraper
13x9-inch pan
pot holders
mixing bowl
mixing spoon
utility fork

HOW TO MAKE IT:

1. Combine cake mix, pudding mix, eggs, 1 cup water and the oil in large mixer bowl; blend well. Then beat at medium speed of electric mixer for 4 minutes.
2. Pour into greased and floured 13x9-inch pan. Bake at 350° for 45 to 50 minutes, or until cake springs back when lightly touched. Cool in pan about 15 minutes.
3. Meanwhile, dissolve gelatin in boiling water; add cold water.
4. Poke holes in warm cake with utility fork at ½-inch intervals.
5. Carefully pour gelatin over cake. Chill 3 to 4 hours.
6. Cut into squares and top with prepared Dream Whip whipped topping, if desired. Makes 12 to 15 servings.

◆Spicy Apple-cadabra

THESE GO IN:

1 package (3 oz.) Jell-O brand
  raspberry flavor gelatin
1 cup boiling water
¼ cup cold water
1 cup applesauce
½ teaspoon ground cinnamon
1 cup prepared Dream Whip
  whipped topping or thawed
  Birds Eye Cool Whip non-dairy
  whipped topping

GET THESE READY:

mixing bowl
1-cup liquid measure
rubber scraper
measuring spoons
1-cup dry measure
mixing spoon
4 dessert glasses

HOW TO MAKE IT:

1. Dissolve gelatin in boiling water;
   add cold water.
2. Measure 1 cup of the gelatin;
   add applesauce and cinnamon.
3. Spoon into 4 dessert glasses;
   chill 30 minutes.
4. Chill remaining gelatin until
   slightly thickened; blend in
   whipped topping. Spoon over
   applesauce mixture in glasses.
   Garnish with apple wedges, if
   desired. Makes about 3 cups or
   4 servings.

♥Yogurt Whiz

THESE GO IN:
1 cup cold milk
1 container (8 oz.) plain yogurt
1 package (4-serving size)
Jell-O brand instant pudding
and pie filling, any flavor

GET THESE READY:
mixing bowl
1-cup liquid measure
hand beater
rubber scraper
4 dessert dishes

HOW TO MAKE IT:
1. Combine milk and yogurt in mixing bowl.
2. Add pudding mix and beat slowly with hand beater until blended, about 2 minutes.
3. Pour into dessert dishes and let stand for 5 minutes.
4. Chill or serve at once. Garnish with names, using Post Alpha-Bits cereal. Makes about 2 cups or 4 servings.

◆Gelatin Gems

THESE GO IN:
1 package (3 oz.) Jell-O brand
   gelatin, any flavor
1 cup boiling water
¾ cup cold water
1 package (4-serving size)
   Jell-O brand vanilla flavor
   instant pudding and pie filling
2 cups milk

GET THESE READY:
small mixing bowl
1-cup liquid measure
rubber scraper
8-inch square pan
small knife
metal spatula
hand beater or electric mixer
large spoon
6 to 8 dessert glasses

HOW TO MAKE IT:
1. Dissolve gelatin in boiling water;
   add cold water.
2. Pour into an 8-inch square pan.
   Chill until firm, about 3 hours.
   Cut into ½-inch cubes.
3. Pile half the gelatin cubes
   lightly in dessert glasses to fill
   about one-third full.
4. Prepare pudding mix with milk
   as directed on package for
   pudding.
5. Spoon over gelatin cubes and
   top with remaining cubes.
   Makes about 4 cups or 6 to 8
   servings.

◆Boston Cream Parfait

THESE GO IN:
1 package (4-serving size)
  Jell-O brand vanilla flavor
  instant pudding and pie filling
2 cups cold milk
2 tablespoons chocolate syrup
1 cup thawed Birds Eye Cool
  Whip non-dairy whipped
  topping or prepared Dream
  Whip whipped topping

GET THESE READY:
mixing bowl
1-cup liquid measure
rubber scraper
1-cup dry measure
measuring spoons
3 teaspoons
6 parfait glasses

HOW TO MAKE IT:
1. Prepare pudding mix with milk as directed on package for pudding.
2. Pour half the pudding into 6 parfait glasses.
3. Top with chocolate syrup, whipped topping and remaining pudding mixture, spooning chocolate syrup along edge of glass. Chill.
4. Garnish with additional whipped topping, if desired. Makes about 3 cups or 6 servings.

◆Peachy Wizard

THESE GO IN:
1 can (8¾ oz.) sliced peaches
  Cold milk
1 package (4-serving size)
  Jell-O brand vanilla flavor
  instant pudding and pie filling

GET THESE READY:
small bowl
strainer
paring knife

1- or 2-cup liquid measure
mixing bowl
hand beater or
  electric mixer
rubber scraper
5 dessert dishes

HOW TO MAKE IT:
1. Drain peaches, reserving syrup.
   Add cold milk to syrup to make
   2 cups. Set aside 5 slices for
   garnish, if desired; dice
   remaining peaches.

2. Pour measured liquid into a
   deep narrow-bottom bowl. Add
   pudding mix.
3. Beat slowly with hand beater
   or at lowest speed of electric
   mixer until well blended, about
   2 minutes.
4. Quickly stir in peaches and
   pour at once into individual
   dessert dishes. Let stand to set,
   about 5 minutes. Garnish with
   reserved peach slices. Makes
   about 2½ cups or 5 servings.

Snacks.

You can be a magician and, presto, make snacks for the whole family. When the kids come in from school, Jell-O brand gelatin and pudding make you a real wizard at turning out delicious snacks.

Marvello's French Drop

YOU'LL NEED:

1 nickel

Magicians say this is one of their basic skills. Whenever you see a magician make something small disappear, you can be sure the "French Drop" has been used.

Hold a nickel between the thumb and forefinger of your left hand, with the *back* of your hand facing the audience. Reach for the coin with your right hand, so that your thumb goes under the coin in the circle made by the left thumb and forefinger. Now, lift your right hand up and away, closing your fingers into a fist. It should look as though you've taken the nickel into your right hand. But instead, you released the nickel and let it fall into your left palm! As you cup the nickel securely in your palm, drop that hand to your side. You will really fool your audience if you look at your right hand very hard all the while because an audience's eyes are always drawn to whatever the magician is looking at. If you practice this trick over and over, you will be able to make all sorts of objects appear and disappear in a most mysterious way.

♥Root Beer Fizz

THESE GO IN:
1 package (3 oz.) Jell-O brand
  lemon flavor gelatin
1 cup boiling root beer
1½ cups crushed ice

GET THESE READY:
1-cup liquid measure
small saucepan
electric blender
4 glasses
8 straws

HOW TO MAKE IT:
1. Combine gelatin and boiling
   root beer in electric blender
   container.
2. Cover and blend at low speed
   until gelatin is dissolved, about
   1 minute.
3. Add crushed ice and blend at
   high speed until ice is melted,
   about 30 seconds.
4. Pour into 6-ounce soda glasses
   and insert straws. Makes about
   3 cups or 4 servings.
   Note: To crush ice cubes, place
   in canvas or plastic bag and
   pound with mallet or hammer.

♥Puddin' Pops

THESE GO IN:
1 package (4-serving size) Jell-O brand instant pudding and pie filling, any flavor
2 cups cold milk or half and half

GET THESE READY:
2-cup liquid measure
small mixing bowl
hand beater or electric mixer
rubber scraper
six 5-ounce paper cups

6 wooden sticks or plastic spoons, foil or wax paper

HOW TO MAKE IT:
1. Prepare pudding mix with milk as directed on package for pudding. Pour into six 5-ounce paper cups.
2. Insert wooden stick or plastic spoon into each for a handle. Press a square of aluminum foil or wax paper down onto pudding to cover, piercing center of foil square with handle.
3. Freeze until firm, at least 5 hours.
4. Press firmly on bottom of cup to release pop. Serve plain or dip in melted chocolate and sprinkles, if desired. Makes 6 pops.
To melt chocolate: Combine ½ cup Baker's chocolate flavor baking chips and 2 tablespoons water in a saucepan and cook and stir until chocolate is melted and mixture is smooth.

♥Fruity Pops

THESE GO IN:
1 package (3 oz.) Jell-O brand
    gelatin, any flavor
½ cup sugar
2 cups boiling water
2 cups cold water

GET THESE READY:
mixing bowl
½-cup dry measure
1-cup liquid measure
mixing spoon
8 (5-oz.) paper cups or
    9 pop molds
wooden (or plastic)
    spoons or sticks

HOW TO MAKE IT:
1. Dissolve gelatin and sugar in
    boiling water. Add cold water.
2. Pour into plastic or paper cups,
    or pop molds:
    Freeze until almost firm, about
    2 hours.
3. Insert wooden spoons or sticks,
    or plastic spoons. Freeze until
    firm, 8 hours or overnight.
4. Remove cups and sprinkle with
    multicolored sprinkles, if
    desired. Makes about 4 cups
    (or 8 or 9) pops.

★Spicy Apple Cake

THESE GO IN:

1 package (2-layer size) yellow cake mix
1 package (4-serving size) Jell-O brand vanilla flavor instant pudding and pie filling
4 eggs
1 cup applesauce
½ cup water
¼ cup oil
½ teaspoon ground cinnamon
½ teaspoon ground nutmeg
¼ teaspoon ground allspice
½ cup raisins, chopped (optional)

GET THESE READY:

electric mixer
large mixing bowl
rubber scraper
1-cup liquid measure
measuring spoons
1-cup dry measure
13x9-inch pan
cake tester
pot holders
cake rack

HOW TO MAKE IT:

1. Combine all ingredients in large mixer bowl.*
2. Blend well, then beat at medium speed of electric mixer for 4 minutes.
3. Pour into a greased and floured 13x9-inch pan.
4. Bake at 350° for 45 to 50 minutes, or until cake tester inserted in center comes out clean and cake begins to pull away from sides of pan. *Do not underbake.*
5. Cool in pan 15 minutes. Remove from pan and finish cooling on rack.
6. Sprinkle with confectioners sugar, if desired.
   *In high altitude areas, use large eggs, add ¼ cup all-purpose flour and increase water to ⅔ cup.

★Fantastic Fruit Bars

THESE GO IN:

1 cup graham cracker or vanilla wafer crumbs
¼ cup melted butter or margarine
2 packages (3 oz. each) Jell-O brand orange, lemon or peach flavor gelatin*
1 cup boiling water
½ cup light corn syrup
1 cup chopped dried apricots or prunes or chopped mixed dried fruits*
1 teaspoon grated lemon or orange rind (optional)*

GET THESE READY:

1-cup dry measure
1-cup liquid measure
small saucepan
medium bowl
measuring spoons
9-inch square pan
small knife

HOW TO MAKE IT:

1. Combine crumbs and melted butter; sprinkle ½ cup crumb mixture over bottom of a 9-inch square pan.
2. Dissolve gelatin in boiling water.
3. Stir in corn syrup, fruit and rind. Chill until slightly thickened.
4. Pour into pan over crumbs; sprinkle with remaining crumbs. Chill until firm, about 3 hours.
5. Cut into bars; store in refrigerator. (Bars hold well at room temperature for several hours.) Makes 20 confections.

Suggested combinations:
Orange flavor gelatin with apricots and orange rind.
Lemon flavor gelatin with prunes and lemon rind.
Peach flavor gelatin with mixed fruits; omit rind.

◆Creamy Delicious Banana Splits

THESE GO IN:
1 package (4-serving size)
  Jell-O brand banana cream
  or vanilla flavor pudding and
  pie filling
2 cups milk
4 bananas
  Fresh fruit,
  Prepared Dream Whip
    whipped topping,
  Chopped nuts

GET THESE READY:
medium saucepan
1- or 2-cup
liquid measure
mixing spoon
wax paper
paring knife
4 oblong serving dishes

HOW TO MAKE IT:
1. Prepare pudding mix with milk
   as directed on package for
   pudding. Cover with wax paper
   and chill.
2. Cut bananas in half lengthwise
   and arrange in banana split
   dishes.
3. Spoon on pudding, allowing ½
   cup per serving. Top with fruit,
   whipped topping and nuts.
   Makes 4 servings.

◆Hocus-Pocus Banana Splits

THESE GO IN:
1 package (3 oz.) Jell-O brand
  gelatin, any flavor
1 cup boiling water
¾ cup cold water
4 bananas
1 cup thawed Birds Eye Cool
  Whip non-dairy whipped
  topping*
½ cup chopped nuts
  *Or use 1 cup prepared
  Dream Whip whipped
  topping.

GET THESE READY:
mixing bowl
1-cup liquid measure
mixing spoon
8- or 9-inch square pan
dinner fork or ricer
paring knife
4 oblong serving dishes

HOW TO MAKE IT:
1. Dissolve gelatin in boiling water.
  Add cold water.
2. Pour into a shallow pan; chill
   until firm.
3. Break into small flakes with a
   fork, or force through potato
   ricer or large-meshed strainer.
4. Split bananas lengthwise and
   arrange in 4 oblong serving
   dishes.
5. Top with flaked gelatin. Garnish
   with whipped topping and
   sprinkle with nuts. Top with
   maraschino cherries, if desired.
   Makes 4 servings.

♦Frozen Pudding-wiches

THESE GO IN:
1½ cups cold milk
½ cup creamy or chunky peanut butter
1 package (4-serving size) Jell-O brand vanilla or chocolate flavor instant pudding and pie filling
24 graham crackers, sugar honey graham crackers or chocolate wafers

GET THESE READY:
½-cup dry measure
1- or 2-cup liquid measure
small mixing bowl
hand beater or electric mixer
rubber scraper
table knife or small metal spatula

HOW TO MAKE IT:
1. Add milk gradually to peanut butter in a bowl, blending until smooth.
2. Add pudding mix. Beat slowly with hand beater or at lowest speed of electric mixer until well blended, about 2 minutes. Let stand 5 minutes.
3. Spread filling about ½ inch thick on 12 of the crackers.
4. Top with remaining crackers, pressing lightly and smoothing around edges with spatula. Freeze until firm, about 3 hours. Makes 12 sandwiches.

Marvello's Balancing Card Trick

YOU'LL NEED:
1 plastic glass
1 playing card
water

It is very easy to balance a glass of water on a playing card once you know the secret; but you must pretend to your audience that you are doing something difficult and mysterious. Take a light plastic glass with a little water in it. (The water is used to make everyone a little nervous about spilling!) Try to balance the glass on the edge of an ordinary playing card which you are holding sidewise on the edges between your thumb and third finger. Make it look hard. Work at finding the exact point of balance. The trick is that your first finger (pointer) will be up at the top of the card, helping you to hold the glass in place!

♥Gelatin Jiggles

THESE GO IN:
2½ cups boiling water
4 packages (3 oz. each) Jell-O brand gelatin, any flavor

GET THESE READY:
mixing bowl
mixing spoon

1-cup liquid measure
8- or 9-inch square pan
small knife

HOW TO MAKE IT:
1. Add boiling water to gelatin in a bowl and stir until completely dissolved.
2. Pour into an 8-inch square pan.

Chill until firm, about 4 hours.
3. Cut into 1-inch squares. Insert wooden skewers into gelatin, adding miniature marsh-mallows, if desired. Makes 64 candies.

Note: Mixture may be chilled in a 9-inch square pan; makes 81 candies.

♥Smilin' Snacks

THESE GO IN:

1 package (4-serving size)
Jell-O brand instant pudding
and pie filling, any flavor
2 cups milk
garnishes

GET THESE READY:
electric mixer or hand beater
small mixing bowl
mixing spoon
1-cup liquid measure
4 paper cups

HOW TO MAKE IT:

1. Prepare instant pudding with
milk as directed on package
for pudding.
2. Let stand for 5 minutes; then
spoon into 5-ounce paper cups.
3. Make "faces" with gumdrops,
jelly beans, raisins, Baker's
Angel Flake coconut,
cinnamon candies, miniature
marshmallows, cereal or
Baker's chocolate flavor baking
chips. Makes 2 cups or 4
servings.

★Bewitched Brownies

THESE GO IN:
1 package (4-serving size)
  Jell-O brand chocolate fudge,
  chocolate, or milk chocolate
  flavor pudding and pie filling*
½ cup all-purpose flour*
¼ teaspoon Calumet baking
  powder
⅓ cup butter or margarine
⅔ cup sugar
2 eggs
1 teaspoon vanilla
½ cup chopped walnuts

*Or use 1 package (4-serving
 size) Jell-O brand chocolate
 or chocolate fudge flavor instant
 pudding and pie filling; reduce
 flour to ⅓ cup.

GET THESE READY:
mixing bowl
small saucepan
1 set measuring cups
hand beater or
  electric mixer
measuring spoons
mixing spoon
8-inch square pan
cake rack

HOW TO MAKE IT:
1. Combine pudding mix, flour
   and baking powder; mix well.
2. Melt butter in saucepan,
   remove from heat and add
   sugar.
3. Beat in eggs, one at a time.
4. Blend in vanilla and pudding
   mixture; stir in nuts.
5. Spread in a greased 8-inch
   square pan.
6. Bake at 350° for 35 minutes.
7. Cool in pan; then cut into bars.
   Makes about 18.

♥Gelatin Cups

THESE GO IN:
1 package (3 oz.) Jell-O brand
   strawberry flavor gelatin
1 cup boiling water
1 cup cold water
4 flat-bottom wafer cones or
   three or four paper cups
½ cup thawed Birds Eye Cool
   Whip non-dairy whipped
   topping

GET THESE READY:
mixing bowl
1-cup liquid measure
mixing spoon

HOW TO MAKE IT:
1. Dissolve gelatin in boiling
   water.
2. Add cold water and chill in
   bowl until set.
3. Spoon set gelatin into wafer
   cones.
4. Top with dollops of whipped
   topping and multicolored
   sprinkles or fruit, if desired.
   Makes 3 or 4 servings.

◆Gelatin-wiches

THESE GO IN:
1 package (3 oz.) Jell-O brand
  peach flavor gelatin
1 cup boiling water
1 container (4½ oz.) Birds Eye
  Cool Whip non-dairy whipped
  topping, thawed
14 double graham crackers,
  separated

GET THESE READY:
mixing bowl
1-cup liquid measure
mixing spoon
small metal spatula

HOW TO MAKE IT:
1. Dissolve gelatin in boiling water
   and chill until slightly thickened.
2. Fold in whipped topping.
3. Spread gelatin mixture about ½
   inch thick on 14 of the crackers;
   top with remaining crackers,
   pressing lightly and smoothing
   around edges with spatula.
4. Freeze until firm, about 3 hours.
   Makes 14 sandwiches.

★Magic Letter Balls

THESE GO IN:
½ cup light corn syrup
¼ cup sugar
1 package (3 oz.) Jell-O brand
  gelatin, any flavor
¾ cup raisins or salted peanuts*
4 cups Post Alpha-Bits
  cereal*

  *Or omit peanuts or raisins and
  use 5 cups Post Alpha-Bits
  cereal.

GET THESE READY:
small saucepan
mixing spoon
1-cup, ½-cup and
  ¼-cup dry measures
2-quart mixing bowl
plastic wrap

HOW TO MAKE IT:
1. Combine syrup, sugar and gelatin in a saucepan.
2. Stir over low heat until sugar and gelatin are *thoroughly* dissolved, about 5 minutes.
3. Combine raisins and cereal in a bowl. Add gelatin mixture, mixing well.
4. Moisten hands in cold water and form cereal mixture into 2-inch balls.
5. Wrap each individually in plastic wrap. Makes about 2 dozen confections.

♥Marvello's Cone Surprise

THESE GO IN:
1 cup cold milk
1 package (4-serving size) Jell-O brand chocolate or vanilla flavor instant pudding and pie filling
1 cup thawed Birds Eye Cool Whip non-dairy whipped topping
¼ cup chopped nuts (optional)
5 flat-bottom wafer cones

GET THESE READY:
small mixing bowl
electric mixer or hand beater
rubber scraper
1-cup liquid measure
1-cup dry measure
¼-cup dry measure
scoop

HOW TO MAKE IT:
1. Pour milk into bowl; add pudding mix.
2. Beat slowly with hand beater or at low speed of electric mixer until well blended, 1 to 2 minutes.
3. Blend in whipped topping; add nuts and chill.
4. Just before serving, scoop pudding mixture into wafer cones.
5. Garnish with additional nuts or chocolate sprinkles, if desired. Makes about 2½ cups or 5 servings.

★Pastel Cupcakes

THESE GO IN:

1 package (2-layer size) white cake mix
1 package (3 oz.) Jell-O brand gelatin, any flavor
¼ cup boiling water
6 tablespoons butter or margarine
3 cups confectioners sugar

GET THESE READY:
electric mixer and large bowl
1-cup liquid measure
rubber scraper
mixing spoon
cupcake pans and liners
1-quart bowl
measuring spoons
1-cup dry measure
small metal spatula

HOW TO MAKE IT:

1. Prepare cake mix as directed on package for cupcakes, adding ½ package (about 4 tablespoons) of the gelatin before beating.
2. Cool 10 minutes in pans. Remove from pans and finish cooling on racks.
3. Dissolve remaining gelatin in the boiling water.
4. Cream butter; add part of the sugar gradually, blending after each addition. Add remaining sugar alternately with gelatin mixture, beating until smooth.
5. Spread on tops of cupcakes. Makes 2 to 2½ dozen cupcakes and about 1¾ cups frosting. *To make gumdrop flower garnish:* cut large gumdrop to resemble a tulip. Insert wooden pick into flower; attach gumdrop strip for a stem. Attach flattened gumdrop pieces for leaves.

◆Fanciful Fudge

THESE GO IN:

1 package (4-serving size)
  Jell-O brand chocolate, milk
  chocolate, or chocolate fudge
  flavor pudding and pie filling
¼ cup milk
2 tablespoons butter or margarine
2 cups sifted confectioners sugar
¼ cup chopped nuts

GET THESE READY:

medium saucepan
mixing spoon
loaf pan
wax paper
1-cup liquid measure
1-cup dry measure
small knife

HOW TO MAKE IT:

1. Combine pudding mix and milk
   in a saucepan; add butter.
2. Bring to a boil over medium
   heat, stirring constantly. Remove
   from heat.
3. Stir in sugar and beat until
   smooth; add nuts.
4. Quickly pour into a greased or
   wax paper-lined 8x4- or 9x5-
   inch loaf pan. Chill until firm,
   about 30 minutes.
5. Cut into pieces. Store, covered,
   in refrigerator. Stack on a plate
   to resemble a fort; add a paper
   flag, if desired.

Marvello's Upside-Down Trick

YOU'LL NEED.

1 glass
1 piece of cardboard — slightly larger than the rim of the glass
water

Practice this trick over a sink, or you may wind up with a big puddle! First, fill the glass with water *all the way up to the top*, so there are no air bubbles. This is very important, because if there are any air bubbles, the trick will not work. Take the cardboard and place it over the top of the glass, holding it flat with the palm of your hand. Turn the glass upside down *slowly*, still holding the card in place. When you have turned the glass all the way over, check to see there are no air bubbles. Then take your hand away and neither the card nor the water will fall. Amazing!

Holiday Desserts.

A holiday is a time for families. That's when everyone comes together to remember old traditions and to begin new ones. That's when Jell-O brand gelatin and pudding help both parents and children create magical holiday traditions of their own.

◆Christmas Tree Cake

THESE GO IN:
1 package (2-layer size) yellow cake mix
1 package (4-serving size) Jell-O brand pistachio flavor instant pudding and pie filling
4 eggs
1¼ cups water
¼ cup oil
½ teaspoon almond extract
7 drops green food coloring (optional)
Fluffy Vanilla Frosting
Baker's Angel Flake coconut, tinted green
Gumdrops

GET THESE READY:
electric mixer
large mixing bowl
rubber scraper
1-cup liquid measure
measuring spoons
13x9-inch pan
pot holders
cake tester
cake rack

HOW TO MAKE IT:
1. Combine cake mix, pudding mix, eggs, water, oil, extract and coloring in large mixer bowl.*
2. Blend; then beat at medium speed of electric mixer for 4 minutes.
3. Pour into a greased and floured 13x9-inch pan.
4. Bake at 350° for 40 to 45 minutes, or until cake tester inserted in center comes out clean and cake begins to pull away from sides of pan. *Do not underbake.*
5. Cool in pan about 15 minutes. Remove from pan and finish cooling on rack.
6. Frost top and sides with Fluffy Vanilla Frosting (p. 93). Mark shape of Christmas tree and sprinkle with tinted coconut. Decorate with gumdrops.
*In high altitude areas, use large eggs, add ¼ cup all-purpose flour and increase water to 1½ cup.

★Santa's Stocking

THESE GO IN:
1 baked 13x9-inch white or yellow cake, cooled
1 package (3 oz.) Jell-O brand strawberry flavor gelatin
1¼ cups boiling water
1 package (10 oz.) Birds Eye quick thaw strawberries
1 container (9 oz.) Birds Eye Cool Whip non-dairy whipped topping

GET THESE READY:
wooden picks
sharp knife
2 platters or 1 large tray
aluminum foil
mixing bowl
1-cup liquid measure
mixing spoon
metal spatula

HOW TO MAKE IT:
1. Cut cake as shown in Diagram 1. For ease in cutting, first measure and mark distances with wooden picks; then cut between picks with a sharp knife.
2. Place pieces on two platters, or a large tray. Trim off corners, as shown in Diagram 2 to form toes and heels of stockings. Secure 3-inch strips of aluminum foil to sides of cakes with wooden picks to form a collar.
3. Dissolve gelatin in boiling water. Add frozen fruit; stir gently until fruit thaws and separates, and gelatin is slightly thickened.
4. Select Post Alpha-Bits cereal to form a name if desired, and dip letters into gelatin to coat lightly. Chill.
5. Spoon remaining gelatin onto cakes. Chill until firm, about 1 hour.
6. Carefully remove foil strips. Frost sides of cakes and the cuff, heel and toe areas with whipped topping as shown in Diagram 3. Place "name" on cuffs. Makes about 12 to 14 servings.

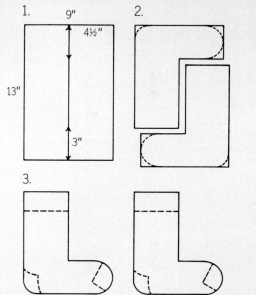

◆ Peter Pumpkin Mousse

THESE GO IN:
1 package (4-serving size) Jell-O brand butterscotch or vanilla flavor instant pudding and pie filling
1¼ cups cold milk
1 cup canned pumpkin
¼ teaspoon ground cinnamon
¼ teaspoon ground nutmeg
¼ teaspoon ground ginger
1 cup thawed Birds Eye Cool Whip non-dairy whipped topping

GET THESE READY:
electric mixer or hand beater
small mixing bowl
1-cup liquid measure
1-cup dry measure
measuring spoons
rubber scraper
tablespoon
5 dessert glasses

HOW TO MAKE IT:
1. Combine pudding mix, milk, pumpkin and spices in small mixing bowl.
2. Beat until well blended.
3. Fold in whipped topping; spoon into dessert glasses. Garnish with additional whipped topping and candy corn, if desired. Makes 2½ cups or 5 servings.

◆Bunny Mousse

THESE GO IN:

1 package (4-serving size)
  Jell-O brand pistachio flavor
  instant pudding and pie filling
1½ cups cold milk
1 cup thawed Birds Eye Cool
  Whip non-dairy whipped
  topping

GET THESE READY:

electric mixer or
  hand beater
small mixing bowl
1-cup liquid measure
1-cup dry measure
rubber scraper
tablespoon
5 dessert glasses

HOW TO MAKE IT:

1. Prepare pudding mix with milk
   as directed on package for
   pudding.
2. Fold in whipped topping and
   spoon into dessert dishes.
3. Garnish with marshmallow
   bunny face, if desired. Makes
   about 2½ cups or 5 servings.

To make bunny face: Insert
wooden picks into miniature
marshmallows; attach to large
marshmallow to resemble ears.
Add a face, using cut pieces of
small gumdrops; add broken
wooden picks for whiskers.
Attach to large marshmallow,
turned sideways.

80

◆Halloween Pie

THESE GO IN:
1 package (6-serving size) Jell-O brand vanilla flavor instant pudding and pie filling
1 can (16 oz.) pumpkin
1 cup cold milk
½ teaspoon ground nutmeg*
½ teaspoon ground ginger*
½ teaspoon ground cinnamon*
1 baked 9-inch graham cracker crumb crust, cooled
1 container (4½ oz.) Birds Eye Cool Whip non-dairy whipped topping, thawed

*Or use 1 teaspoon pumpkin pie spice.

GET THESE READY:
9-inch pie plate
mixing bowl
mixing spoon
electric mixer or hand beater
1-cup liquid measure
1-cup dry measure
measuring spoons
wax paper
metal spatula

HOW TO MAKE IT:
1. Combine pie filling mix, pumpkin, milk and spices in bowl.
2. Mix slowly with electric mixer or hand beater just until blended, about 1 minute.
3. Fold in 1 cup of the whipped topping.
4. Spoon into pie shell. Chill until set, at least 2 hours.
5. Garnish with remaining whipped topping. (To make "face," cut pieces of wax paper in shape of eyes, nose and mouth and place on pie filling. Spread whipped topping around papers; then remove papers. Garnish with candy corn to resemble teeth.)

♦Jack O'Lantern Cake

THESE GO IN:

1 baked 9-inch cake layer, cooled
1 package (3 oz.) Jell-O brand orange flavor gelatin
1¼ cups boiling water
1 can (8 oz.) crushed pineapple in juice
1 container (4½ oz.) Birds Eye Cool Whip non-dairy whipped topping

GET THESE READY:

aluminum foil
wooden picks
small mixing bowl
can opener
1-cup liquid measure
rubber scraper
mixing spoon
wax paper
metal spatula

HOW TO MAKE IT:

1. Place cake layer on a plate or tray; secure 3-inch strips of aluminum foil to sides of cake with wooden picks to form a collar.
2. Dissolve gelatin in boiling water. Add pineapple with juice and chill until slightly thickened.
3. Spoon over top of cake and chill until firm, about 3 hours. Carefully remove foil strips.
4. Cut out a pumpkin face from a 9-inch round of wax paper and set on gelatin.
5. Spread whipped topping over openings in paper and around sides of cake. Remove paper. Makes 8 servings.

★Ginger Men

THESE GO IN:
1½ cups all-purpose flour
½ teaspoon baking soda
1½ teaspoons ground ginger
1 teaspoon ground cinnamon
½ cup butter or other shortening
½ cup firmly packed brown sugar
1 package (4-serving size)
   Jell-O brand butterscotch
   flavor pudding and pie filling
1 egg

Marvello's Indian Rope Trick

YOU'LL NEED:
1 length of rope

Every magician knows some rope tricks. Here's a simple one which will amaze your friends. Tell them that you can tie a knot in a length of rope without ever taking your hands off it. Cross your arms in front of you so that one hand is in front of your elbow and the other hand is behind the other elbow. Next, hold one end of the rope in each hand. Then uncross your arms, and like magic, you've tied a knot in the rope!

GET THESE READY:

electric mixer with small bowl
rubber scraper
1-cup dry measure
½-cup dry measure
measuring spoons
rolling pin
pastry board
cookie cutters
cake racks
baking sheets
pastry bag with lettering tube

HOW TO MAKE IT:

1. Mix flour with baking soda and spices.
2. Cream butter; beat in sugar and pudding mix. Add egg and blend well.
3. Gradually add flour mixture, beating after each addition until smooth. Chill dough until firm enough to handle.
4. Roll about 1/8 inch thick on floured board. Cut with floured cookie cutter.
5. Place on greased baking sheets. Decorate with raisins, cinnamon candies, candied cherries, nonpareils, or red or green crystal sugar, if desired.
6. Bake at 350° for 10 to 12 minutes. Decorate cooled cookies with glaze, if desired. Makes about 2½ dozen.
   Confectioners Sugar Glaze. Gradually add 1 tablespoon (about) hot milk or water to 1 cup sifted confectioners sugar.

◆Easter Surprise Cake

THESE GO IN:
1 package (2-layer size) yellow cake mix
1 package (4-serving size) Jell-O brand pistachio flavor instant pudding and pie filling
4 eggs
1¼ cups water
¼ cup oil
½ teaspoon almond extract
7 drops green food coloring (optional)
Fluffy Pistachio Frosting
Baker's Angel Flake coconut, tinted green
jelly beans

GET THESE READY:
electric mixer
large mixing bowl
rubber scraper
1-cup liquid measure
measuring spoons
10-inch fluted tube or tube pan
cake tester
pot holders
cake rack

HOW TO MAKE IT:
1. Combine cake mix, pudding mix, eggs, water, oil and extract in large mixer bowl.*
2. Blend; then beat at medium speed of electric mixer for 4 minutes.
3. Pour into a greased and floured 10-inch fluted tube or tube pan.
4. Bake at 350° for 50 to 55 minutes, or until cake tester inserted in center comes out clean and cake begins to pull away from sides of pan. *Do not underbake.*
5. Cool in pan about 15 minutes. Remove from pan and finish cooling on rack.
6. Frost with Fluffy Pistachio Frosting (p. 93), sprinkle coconut around the top and sides and garnish with jelly beans.

*In high altitude areas, use large eggs, add ¼ cup all-purpose flour and increase water to 1½ cups.

◆Dazzling Easter Eggs

THESE GO IN:
8 eggs
1 package (3 oz.) Jell-O brand gelatin, any flavor
1 cup boiling water
½ cup milk

GET THESE READY:
skewer or cake tester
mixing bowl
wire whip or fork
1-cup liquid measure
mixing spoon

HOW TO MAKE IT:
1. Using a skewer or cake tester, make a ½-inch hole in one end of each egg shell. Shake eggs out of shells, reserving 1 egg. (Use remaining eggs at another time.)
2. Rinse shells thoroughly with cold water and place in an egg carton.
3. Beat reserved egg slightly; blend in gelatin. Add boiling water and stir until gelatin is dissolved.
4. Add milk and pour carefully into egg shells. Chill until firm, about 4 hours.
5. Crack shells slightly, dip quickly in warm water and peel off shells.
6. Arrange "eggs" in nests of green-tinted Baker's Angel Flake coconut, if desired. Makes 8 "eggs" or 4 servings.

Party Desserts.

Let's have a party! Balloons, funny hats, magic tricks and party desserts that make everybody happy. Jell-O brand gelatin and pudding add real magic to your parties.

◆Delight Pie

THESE GO IN:
9-inch Chocolate Cookie Crumb Crust
1 package (6-serving size) Jell-O brand chocolate or chocolate fudge flavor instant pudding and pie filling
2½ cups milk
1⅓ cups thawed Birds Eye Cool Whip non-dairy whipped topping

GET THESE READY:
9-inch pie plate
electric mixer or hand beater
mixing bowl
mixing spoon
1-cup liquid measure
1-cup dry measure
⅓-cup dry measure
metal spatula

HOW TO MAKE IT:
1. Prepare pie filling mix with 2½ cups milk as directed on package for pie.
2. Measure 1 cup; pour remaining pie filling into pie crust.
3. Blend whipped topping into measured pie filling.
4. Spread over filling in crust. Chill about 3 hours.
5. Garnish with additional whipped topping and chocolate cookies, cut in quarters, if desired.

For ease in serving, dip pie plate in warm water for a few seconds, then cut and serve.

Chocolate Cookie Crumb Crust: Combine 1¼ cups chocolate or chocolate fudge cookie crumbs and 2 tablespoons sugar. Mix in ¼ cup margarine or butter, melted. Press firmly on bottom and sides of a 9-inch pie plate. Bake at 375° for 8 minutes. Cool.

◆Super Duper Peanut Cake

THESE GO IN:
1 package (2-layer size) yellow cake mix
1 package (4-serving size) Jell-O brand vanilla flavor instant pudding and pie filling
4 eggs
1 cup water
¼ cup oil
1 cup chunky peanut butter
Easy Creamy Frosting
Chopped peanuts
Halved peanuts
Gumdrops

GET THESE READY:
Cake:
electric mixer
large mixer bowl
1-cup liquid measure

rubber scraper
1-cup dry measure
13x9-inch pan
cake tester
cake rack
pot holders
metal spatula
knife
chopping board

Frosting:
1-cup liquid measure
electric mixer
small mixer bowl
rubber scraper
measuring spoon

HOW TO MAKE IT:
1. Combine cake mix, pudding mix, eggs, water, oil and peanut butter in large mixer bowl.*
2. Blend; then beat at medium speed of electric mixer for 4 minutes.

3. Pour into a greased and floured 13x9-inch pan.
4. Bake at 350° for 40 to 45 minutes, or until cake tester inserted in center comes out clean and cake begins to pull away from sides of pan. *Do not underbake.*
5. Cool in pan about 15 minutes. Remove from pan and finish cooling on rack.
6. Frost top and sides with Easy Creamy Frosting. Sprinkle chopped peanuts on sides of cake, and outline dog's head, eyes and mouth with halved peanuts. Add gumdrop eyes, nose and tongue. Store in

refrigerator.
In high altitude areas, use large eggs, add ⅓ cup all-purpose flour and increase water to 1½ cups; bake at 375° for 50 to 55 minutes.

Easy Creamy Frosting:
Pour ⅔ cup milk into small bowl. Add 2 packages (4-serving size) Jell-O brand chocolate flavor instant pudding and pie filling and 1 teaspoon vanilla; stir until smooth. Add ½ cup softened butter or margarine and blend well. Add 4 cups confectioners sugar, stirring until creamy. Makes 3 cups.

★Birthday Book Cake

THESE GO IN:

1 package (2-layer size) lemon cake mix
1 package (4-serving size) Jell-O brand lemon flavor instant pudding and pie filling
4 eggs
1 cup water
¼ cup oil
Easy Creamy Frosting
Yellow, red and green food coloring

GET THESE READY:

electric mixer
large mixer bowl
1-cup liquid measure
rubber scraper
13x9-inch pan
cake tester
cake rack
pot holders
metal spatula
pastry bag with lettering tube
fork
candles

HOW TO MAKE IT:

1. Combine cake mix, pudding mix, eggs, water and oil in large mixer bowl.*
2. Blend; then beat at medium speed of electric mixer for 4 minutes.
3. Pour into greased and floured 13x9-inch pan.

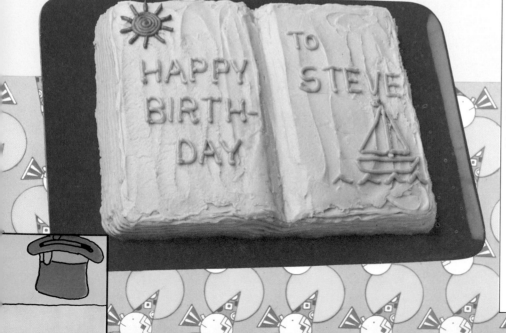

★Gelatin Express

THESE GO IN:

4 packages (3 oz. each) or 2 packages (6 oz. each) Jell-O brand orange flavor gelatin
4 cups boiling water
2½ cups cold water
6 baked cupcakes, cooled
2½ cups thawed Birds Eye Cool Whip non-dairy whipped topping
Small and large gumdrops
1 large marshmallow
4 vanilla wafers

GET THESE READY:

mixing bowl
rubber scraper
1- or 2-cup liquid measure
9x5-inch loaf pan

4. Bake at 350° for 45 to 50 minutes, or until cake tester inserted in center comes out clean and cake begins to pull away from sides of pan. *Do not underbake.*

5. Cool in pan about 15 minutes. Remove from pan and finish cooling on rack.

6. Place cake top-side down on large tray.

7. Make a cut, about ¾ inch deep down center of cake; cut and remove 2 wedge-shaped pieces.

8. Round off the short edges of cake to resemble an open book.

9. Tint 1¼ cups of the frosting with yellow food coloring; tint ¼ cup with green food coloring and tint 2 tablespoons orange with red and yellow food coloring.

10. Spread untinted frosting smoothly over top of cake.

11. Frost sides with yellow frosting; let set for a few minutes; then mark with 4-tined fork to resemble pages of book.

12. Using pastry bag with plain tube, pipe on lettering and a design with green frosting, adding the orange frosting to the design.

13. Arrange candles on cake.

In high altitude areas, use large eggs, add ¼ cup all-purpose flour and increase water to 1½ cups; bake for 55 minutes.

Easy Creamy Frosting: See pg 89, use Jell-O brand lemon flavor instant pudding and pie filling.

metal spatula
1-cup dry measure
paring knife
tray or platter

HOW TO MAKE IT:

1. Dissolve gelatin in boiling water. Add cold water and pour into 9x5-inch loaf pan.

2. Chill overnight until very firm. Unmold onto serving tray.

3. Frost 1 cupcake with whipped topping and decorate with gumdrops to make a face; place in front of gelatin.

4. Arrange remaining cupcakes on top of gelatin. Frost with whipped topping and decorate with gumdrops and marshmallow. Attach wafers and gumdrops for wheels.

◆Double Delight Cones

THESE GO IN:
1 package (3 oz.) Jell-O brand chocolate flavor pudding and pie filling
1¾ cups milk
1 package (1-layer size) yellow cake mix
1 egg
½ cup milk or water
9 flat-bottom wafer cones

GET THESE READY:
saucepan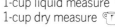
1-cup liquid measure
mixing spoon
electric mixer with small bowl
measuring spoons
baking sheet
cake rack

HOW TO MAKE IT:
1. Prepare pudding mix as directed on package for pudding, reducing milk to 1¾ cups; cool.
2. Prepare cake mix with egg and ½ cup milk as directed on package.
3. Spoon about 1 tablespoon cake batter into bottom of each cone.
4. Top with 1 tablespoon pudding and add 2 tablespoons cake batter.
5. Set cones on a baking sheet and bake at 350° for 25 minutes.
6. Cool on a rack. (Chill remaining pudding for another dessert.)
7. Frost with prepared butter cream frosting and top with chocolate sprinkles, if desired. Makes 9 cones.

★Magic Dot Cake

THESE GO IN:
1 package (2-layer size) chocolate cake mix
1 package (4-serving size) Jell-O brand chocolate flavor instant pudding and pie filling
4 eggs
1 cup water
¼ cup oil
Quick Fluffy Frosting

GET THESE READY:
Cake:
electric mixer
large mixer bowl
1-cup liquid measure
rubber scraper
cake tester
cake rack
pot holders
wax paper
wooden picks
pastry bag with lettering tube
metal spatula
Frosting:
small bowl
1-cup liquid measure
1-cup dry measure

measuring spoons
mixing spoon

HOW TO MAKE IT:

1. Combine cake mix, pudding mix, eggs, water and oil in large mixer bowl.*
2. Blend; then beat at medium speed of electric mixer for 4 minutes.
3. Pour into a greased and floured 13x9-inch pan.
4. Bake at 350° for 40 to 45 minutes, or until cake tester inserted in center comes out clean and cake begins to pull away from sides of pan. *Do not underbake.*
5. Cool in pan about 15 minutes. Remove from pan and finish cooling on rack.
6. Arrange about ten 2x1-inch pieces of wax paper on top of cake; secure with wooden picks.
7. Set aside ⅓ cup of the frosting; spread remaining frosting on sides and top of cake just to edges of wax paper pieces.
8. Remove the wax paper. Using pastry bag with plain tube, pipe lines and dots with reserved frosting on the unfrosted areas to resemble dominos.

In high altitude areas, use devil's food cake mix and large eggs; add ¼ cup all-purpose flour and increase water to 1½ cups; bake 45 to 50 minutes.

Quick Fluffy Frosting:
Pour 1½ cups cold milk into deep narrow-bottom mixer bowl. Add 1 envelope Dream Whip whipped topping mix and 1 package (4-serving size) Jell-O brand vanilla flavor instant pudding and pie filling. Beat slowly until well blended. Gradually increase beating speed to high and whip until mixture will form soft peaks, 4 to 6 minutes. Makes 3 cups.

★Roundabout Cake

THESE GO IN:
1 package (2-layer size) yellow
  cake mix
1 package (4-serving size) Jell-O
  brand vanilla flavor instant
  pudding and pie filling
4 eggs
1 cup water
¼ cup oil
2 squares Baker's unsweetened
  chocolate, melted
  Semi-Sweet Glaze
6 to 8 animal crackers

GET THESE READY: *Cake:*
large mixing bowl
electric mixer
1-cup liquid measure
rubber scraper
10-inch tube or
  fluted tube pan
tablespoon
metal spatula
cake tester
cake rack
pot holders
3 to 4 plastic straws or
  small candles
Glaze:
measuring spoons

small saucepan
rubber scraper
1-cup dry measure
mixing spoon or tablespoon

HOW TO MAKE IT:
1. Combine cake mix, pudding
   mix, eggs, water and oil in large
   mixer bowl.*
2. Blend; then beat at medium
   speed of electric mixer for 4
   minutes.
3. Pour half the batter into a
   greased and floured 10-inch
   tube or fluted tube pan.
4. Blend chocolate into remaining

◆Gingerberry Brew

THESE GO IN:
1 package (3 oz.) Jell-O brand
  strawberry flavor gelatin
½ cup sugar
1½ cups boiling water
2½ cups cold water
1 package (10 oz.) Birds Eye
  quick thaw strawberries
1 can (6 fl. oz.) frozen concentrate
  for limeade or lemonade
3 bottles (12 fl. oz. each)
  ginger ale
Ice cubes
Mint leaves

GET THESE READY:
large mixing bowl

batter. Spoon into pan and cut through with spatula to marble. Bake at 350° for 50 to 55 minutes, or until cake tester inserted in center comes out clean and cake begins to pull away from sides of pan. *Do not underbake.*

5. Cool in pan about 15 minutes. Remove from pan and finish cooling on rack.
6. Spoon glaze over cooled cake; cut straws in half and arrange on top of cake with crackers.
 In high altitude areas, use large eggs, add ¼ cup all-purpose flour and increase water to 1½ cups.

Semi-Sweet Glaze: Place 3 squares Baker's semi-sweet chocolate, 3 tablespoons water and 1 tablespoon butter or margarine in a saucepan. Stir over low heat until chocolate is melted and mixture is smooth. Combine 1 cup sifted confectioners sugar and a dash of salt in small bowl. Gradually blend in chocolate mixture. Makes about ¾ cup.

½-cup dry measure
1- or 2-cup
  liquid measure
mixing spoon
can opener
punch bowl (3-quart)
punch cups

HOW TO MAKE IT:
1. Dissolve gelatin and sugar in boiling water.
2. Add cold water, strawberries and concentrate; stir until berries and concentrate are thawed. Chill.
3. Just before serving, add ginger ale, ice cubes and mint. Serve in punch cups. Makes about 2½ quarts or 20 servings.

Index